ITALY

Gem of the Mediterranean

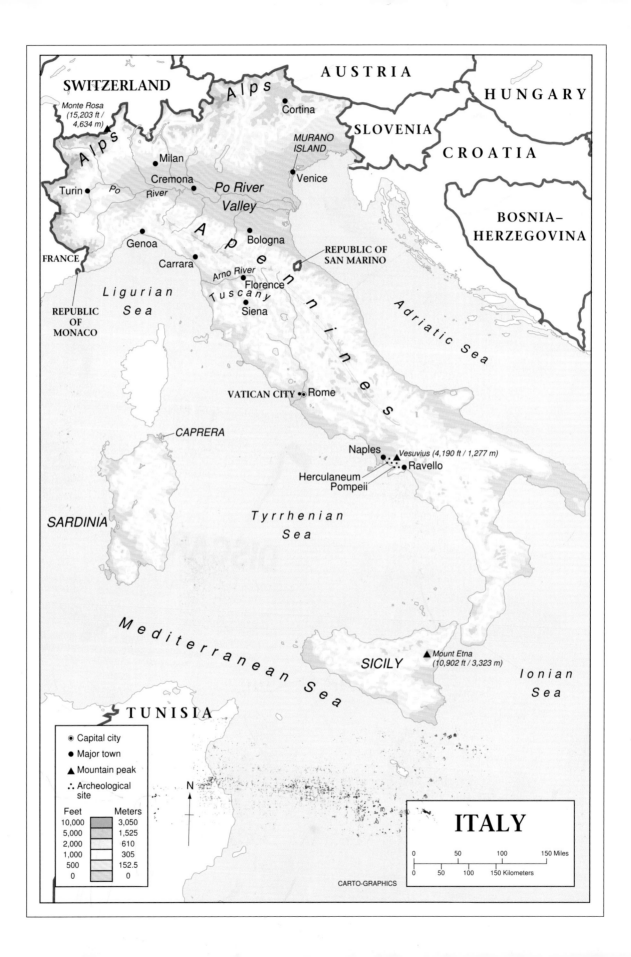

SWITZERLAND

Monte Rosa (15,203 ft / 4,634 m)

Alps

Alps

AUSTRIA

Cortina

HUNGARY

SLOVENIA

MURANO ISLAND

CROATIA

Milan

Cremona

Po River Valley

Venice

Turin

Po

River

BOSNIA–
HERZEGOVINA

FRANCE

Genoa

A p e n n i n e s

Bologna

REPUBLIC OF
SAN MARINO

Carrara

Arno River

Florence

Adriatic Sea

*Ligurian
Sea*

Tuscany

Siena

REPUBLIC
OF
MONACO

VATICAN CITY •• Rome

CAPRERA

Naples

Vesuvius (4,190 ft / 1,277 m)

Ravello

Herculaneum
Pompeii

SARDINIA

*Tyrrhenian
Sea*

M e d i t e r r a n e a n   S e a

SICILY

Mount Etna
(10,902 ft / 3,323 m)

*Ionian
Sea*

TUNISIA

⊙ Capital city

● Major town

▲ Mountain peak

∴ Archeological
site

Feet	Meters
10,000	3,050
5,000	1,525
2,000	610
1,000	305
500	152.5
0	0

N

ITALY

| 0 | 50 | 100 | 150 Miles |

| 0 | 50 | 100 | 150 Kilometers |

CARTO-GRAPHICS

ITALY

Gem of the Mediterranean

David C. King

BENCHMARK BOOKS

MARSHALL CAVENDISH
NEW YORK

With thanks to Lavinia Lorch for her expert assistance. Ms. Lorch received her doctorate in Classics from Columbia University. She was the headmistress of La Scuola New York, a bilingual and bicultural school, and currently heads the English program at the Lycée Français de New York.

To "Queenie" and all the Genovisi clan, for bringing some of Italy's sunshine to America

Benchmark Books
Marshall Cavendish Corporation
99 White Plains Road
Tarrytown, New York 10591-9001

© Marshall Cavendish Corporation 1998

Library of Congress Cataloging-in-Publication Data
King, David C.
    Italy : gem of the Mediterranean / by David C. King
        p.   cm. — (Exploring cultures of the world)
    Includes bibliographical references and index.
    Summary: Discusses the geography, history, economy, culture, and people of Italy.
    ISBN 0-7614-0394-9 (lib. bdg.)
    1. Italy—Juvenile literature. [1. Italy.] I. Title. II. Series.
DG417.K56   1998
945—DC21   97-6452
                                                                                      CIP
                                                                                      AC

Printed in Hong Kong

Series design by Carol Matsuyama

Front cover: Children in traditional costumes
Back cover: Visitors ride in a gondola in Venice.

Photo Credits
Front cover: Leo de Wys, Inc./W. Hile; back cover and pages 24, 26 28–29, 30, 36, 37, 40, 52, 56: ©Beryl Goldberg, photographer; title page and page 39: Leo de Wys, Inc./Steve Vidler; pages 6, 12, 16: North Wind Picture Archives; page 9: Brooks Walker/National Geographic Image Collection; page 11: Joyce Stanton; pages 14–15, 19, 27, 48, 51: ©Blackbirch Press, Inc.; page 17: Nimatallah/Art Resource, NY; page 20: Leo de Wys, Inc./Peter Baker; page 33: O. Louis Mazzatenta/National Geographic Image Collection; page 35: Jonathan Blair/National Geographic Image Collection; page 44: Winifield I. Parks Jr./National Geographic Image Collection; page 47: AP/Wide World Photo; page 50: Scala/Art Resource, NY; page 57: Joseph J. Scherschel/National Geographic Image Collection.

Contents

Italian patriot Giuseppe Garibaldi (left) *greets King Victor Emmanuel II.*

1
GEOGRAPHY AND HISTORY

Italy Past and Present

Garibaldi and His "Thousand Red Shirts"

In the spring of 1860, rumors flew among villagers in the rocky hills of the island of Sicily. "Garibaldi is coming!" the peasants whispered. Garibaldi and his tiny army, the "Thousand Red Shirts," would free the people from centuries of control by foreign rulers. The Sicilians believed this because Garibaldi always fought on the side of the common people.

Born in 1807, Giuseppe Garibaldi had gone to sea as a boy and rose to become a ship's captain. As a young man he joined a movement that was sweeping the Italian Peninsula. Historians call the movement Il Risorgimento, *or "Rising Again." For centuries, Italy had been divided into many different states and regions. Many of them were controlled by foreign countries. The goal of* Il Risorgimento *was to make Italy a united and independent nation.*

In 1834, Garibaldi took part in a rebellion in the northern city of Genoa. When the uprising failed, he fled to South America. For the next twelve years, he fought for independence causes there. He became skilled in the hit-and-run tactics of guerrilla warfare. His courage, combined with his powerful personality, soon made him famous.

Garibaldi returned to Italy in 1848. There, he joined the struggle for independence and unity. His small band of volunteers fought brilliantly against armies of both France and Austria.

Even when he was outnumbered and forced to flee, his escapes added to his fame. His beloved wife and companion-in-arms, Anita, died during one of these escapes.

In May 1860, Garibaldi began his greatest adventure—the invasion of Sicily with only his "Thousand Red Shirts." By this time, most of northern Italy had been united. The southern half of the country still lay under Spanish control. With the support of the Sicilian people, Garibaldi quickly conquered the island. Then he crossed to the mainland and took the city of Naples. The Spanish ruler was forced to flee. Garibaldi was able to turn over all of the south and Sicily to Italy's new king, Victor Emmanuel II. The battle for unity was won.

Garibaldi soon retired to his island of Caprera, off the coast of Sardinia. He is still hailed today as Italy's greatest modern hero.

A Land of Rugged Beauty

Italians often say, "Italy is the most beautiful country in the world." It covers an area no larger than the state of Arizona. But Italy has snow-capped mountains, sparkling lakes, and fertile farm valleys. It has miles of spectacular sandy beaches, graceful harbors, and some of the most famous cities in Europe.

While the landscape is varied and beautiful, it is also a hard land. Rugged mountains and hills cover more than three quarters of the country.

Italy is easy to recognize on a map. The Italian Peninsula is shaped like a ragged boot, jutting from southern Europe into the Mediterranean Sea. The peninsula is surrounded by

The spectacular Alps are the largest mountain range in Europe. They form Italy's northern border with France.

five seas. (Four of the seas are really branches of the fifth, the Mediterranean.)

The toe of Italy's boot looks as if it is about to deliver a kick to Sicily, the largest island in the Mediterranean, and send it spinning toward the island of Sardinia. Both islands are part of Italy.

Europe's tallest mountains—the Alps—are like an umbrella across the north of Italy. Another chain of jagged peaks, called the Apennines, runs like a backbone down the center of the peninsula. It reaches all the way to the heel and toe. Sicily, Sardinia, and about seventy tiny islands stretch along the coast.

A Patchwork of Regions

Italy's geography has had a great influence on the nation's history. The mountains and hills made it difficult for people in different regions to communicate, and a sense of national unity was slow to develop. Even today, many people feel a deeper loyalty to their city or region than to the nation.

There are even two small places within the country's borders that are not part of Italy. One is Vatican City, the home of the Roman Catholic Church. It is located in Rome, Italy's largest city and capital. The other is the tiny mountain republic of San Marino, which lies in the northeastern part of the country.

South of the snow-peaked Alps in the north lies the broad valley of the Po River. This is the flattest area of Italy, and it has the best farmland. Major industries are also located here, especially in the cities of Turin, Milan, and Genoa. Summers in this part of Italy are warm and sunny. Winter, though, brings thick fog, cold rains, and snow.

The central part of Italy is broken up by the Apennines. Two famous cities lie in this area of warmer summers and milder winters. Rome is often called the "Eternal City" because of its proud and ancient history. The other city, Florence, was the center of the great artistic and cultural age known as the Renaissance (REH-nuh-sahns), which began in the 1300s.

The area south of Rome has hot summers and, in the hills, cold winters. The rocky soil makes farming difficult. The very earth there seems to challenge humans. Large earthquakes strike about once every decade, and small ground tremors are common. Southern Italy and the islands also include the only active volcanoes in Europe. The most famous volcano, Vesuvius, rises above the coastal city of Naples. In

The Ponte Vecchio, Florence's famous bridge over the Arno River, dates back to the Middle Ages.

its most powerful eruption, Vesuvius buried the towns of Pompeii and Herculaneum, in the year A.D. 79.

The Long Shadow of History

On a busy street in Rome, workers digging a subway tunnel suddenly stop. Their equipment has struck part of a building foundation far below the street's surface. A crowd gathers. Excitement grows as archaeologists—people who study ancient civilizations—are called in. After weeks of careful excavation, the researchers uncover the ruins of an ancient temple.

Similar stories have been repeated many times in Italy. Modern Italy is continually bumping into reminders of its ancient past.

Ancient Rome

The origins of Italy's civilization, centered in Rome, are shrouded in mystery. Rome was once one of many small farming villages, ruled by a people called the Etruscans. They established a highly advanced society that lasted from the 700s B.C. to the 300s B.C.

Julius Caesar was the greatest leader of the republic of Rome.

Around 500 B.C., the people of Rome overthrew the Etruscans. The Romans were at first ruled by a king, but by 200 B.C. they had established a republic—a government with elected officials. This form of government, in which citizens have a say, was unusual at that time. Romans were proud of it. The republic of Rome expanded. In time, it controlled most of the peninsula. The core of the republic's strength was its army, divided into large fighting units called legions.

The greatest of the republic's leaders was Julius Caesar. He used the legions to conquer new lands. But Julius Caesar destroyed the republic when he declared himself dictator for life. Caesar was murdered in 44 B.C. His grand-nephew soon took the title of "Caesar Augustus," or emperor. The republic of Rome was lost forever.

For the next 200 years, Augustus and his successors increased Rome's holdings. They created the most powerful empire the world had seen.

The Roman Empire established orderly rule and peace throughout the Mediterranean region. Roman law became standard throughout the empire. (It is still the basis for the laws in many modern countries.)

The Romans showed a special genius for engineering. Straight roads and strong bridges, built so that the army could travel rapidly, crisscrossed the empire. Aqueducts—structures made to carry water over long distances—were very sturdy. Enormous arenas, constructed to hold thousands of people, were used for entertainment. One arena, called the Circus Maximus, drew crowds of more than 200,000 to watch chariot races.

The Romans were also skilled in using the ideas of other nations. They borrowed and expanded upon the ideas of the ancient Greeks in art and architecture. Like the Greeks, the Romans built elaborate temples, public baths, and other structures. They also copied Greek styles in poetry and drama.

One famous piece of Roman architecture was the Colosseum. In this large arena, thousands of spectators watched trained fighters called gladiators take on wild animals. The Colosseum was also where the followers of a new religion—Christianity—were sent as punishment to face half-starved lions.

Despite its great power and wealth, the Roman Empire began to crumble. Many of its emperors were weak or corrupt. Agriculture, which was a source of the empire's wealth, declined. At the same time, peoples whom the Romans called "barbarians" began to press into the empire from northern Europe. In A.D. 476, the Roman Empire fell to a barbarian army.

A Divided Land

The centuries that followed the fall of Rome later became known as the Dark Ages. During this time, there was widespread disorder. Fighting, looting, and kidnapping were common. Wealthy people built fortified houses for protection. Nearly all the knowledge of the ancient

The Colosseum was an arena built by the ancient Romans. Today, many visitors to Rome stop at the remains of the enormous structure.

15

Romans and Greeks was lost. A light had gone out in Europe. But this period also saw the spread of Christianity.

Church leaders established Rome as the capital of that faith. The bishop of Rome was eventually named the pope, or father, of the Christian Church. The Christian Church ruled most of central Italy. Parts of northern and all of southern Italy were under foreign control. The Dark Ages gradually gave way to the Middle Ages. This was a period when many great churches and cathedrals were built.

Venice was a rich and important city-state during the Renaissance. In this old picture, you can see the lively activity along the canals, which are the city's streets.

North of the papal lands, independent nobles ruled small areas. Each area was made up of a walled city and its surrounding countryside. Over several centuries, these "city-states" gained in wealth and power.

The prosperity of the city-states contributed to one of the greatest periods of creative energy the world has ever known. It was called the Renaissance, or "Rebirth." Thanks to Irish monks, who preserved ancient Greek and Roman writings in the quiet of their monasteries, the knowledge of earlier times eventually returned to Europe. By the 1300s, people in Italy had rediscovered the art and architecture, science and literature of the Roman Empire. There was a rebirth of culture.

This portrait of Isabella D'Este, one of the most influential women of the Renaissance, was painted by a great artist of the period: Peter Paul Rubens.

The heart of the Italian Renaissance was the city-state of Florence, home to many great artists. The ideas of the Renaissance spread rapidly through Italy and then to most of Europe. Some of the greatest artists the world has ever known, including Michelangelo and Leonardo da Vinci, lived during the Renaissance.

THE GOVERNMENT OF ITALY

Italy is a parliamentary republic. The country is divided into twenty regions, which are similar to the states in the United States except that they have less control over their own affairs.

The national government is made up of three branches: the legislative, executive, and judicial. The legislative, or law-making branch, is the parliament. It is made up of two houses: the Chamber of Deputies, which has 630 members, and the Senate, which has 315 members. Both senators and deputies serve for five years.

In the executive branch, the president is head of state and is elected for a seven-year term by parliament and members of regional councils. The president does not actually run the government. The prime minister, with his cabinet of ministers, is in charge of running the government. The prime minister is chosen by the president and is the leader of the party that has the largest representation in the Chamber of Deputies.

In the judicial branch, there are two main courts. The Supreme Court is the highest court of appeal in all cases except those concerning the Constitution. The Constitutional Court is similar to the Supreme Court of the United States and decides cases concerned with the Constitution. It is made up of fifteen justices.

Citizens must be twenty-five years old to vote for senators; the voting age for all other elected officials is eighteen.

Modern Italy

The Renaissance lasted until about 1600. During that time—and for two centuries after—the Italian Peninsula remained splintered into separate, independent regions. They were often at war with one another. The more powerful nations of France, Spain, and Austria took control of large areas of the Italian Peninsula.

Early in the 1800s, however, the desire for unity and independence grew. Some patriots started a movement that historians call *Il Risorgimento* (ill ree-SOR-jee-men-toh). Soon most of northern Italy was united. In 1860–1861, Giuseppe Garibaldi completed unification with his brilliant conquest of

The beautiful city of Florence has shared in Italy's post-World War II prosperity.

Sicily and southern Italy. The lands of the pope were added a few years later.

For nearly a century following unification, Italy struggled to overcome its deep social divisions and poverty. In the 1920s, the nation fell under the spell of a military dictator, Benito Mussolini. He plunged the country into World War II (1939–1945) on the side of Germany's power-mad dictator, Adolf Hitler. But, during the war, the Italian people drove Mussolini from office, killed him, and joined the other side, the Allies, in ending the war.

After 1945, Italy rose from the ashes of wartime destruction. It was a time of great economic growth and prosperity. In 1946, the nation became a republic. The government, though, remains broken into many political parties. And the head of the government, the prime minister, has changed often. But these problems have not stopped Italians from enjoying their prosperity, which they call *"Il Boom."*

A group of Sicilian musicians entertains from a brightly decorated cart.

2
THE PEOPLE

Meet the Italian People

On a Sunday morning drive to the beach, the residents of an Italian city find themselves trapped in an endless traffic jam. How do they react? Instead of becoming angry, people climb out of their cars and strike up friendly conversations with those around them.

Visitors to Italy are often struck by this fondness for company and conversation. Whether enjoying a four-hour holiday meal, taking an evening stroll, or caught in traffic, the Italian people show a great love of life.

While Italians share these and other traits, there are also sharp differences in people from one region to another. Among these regional differences is the way the Italian language is spoken.

Will You Please Speak Italian?
In the days of the Roman Empire, Latin was the language of the entire peninsula. Roads connected the people. When the empire fell apart, communication between regions became

difficult. As each region developed independently, the language that emerged from the original Latin formed into local dialects. Soon, people in one region could not understand people in another.

In the 1300s, one of the best poets of the period, Dante Alighieri, wrote a masterpiece, *The Divine Comedy*. Rather than write in Latin like other scholars of the period, Dante wrote in his native Tuscan dialect. Boccaccio and other well-known Tuscan poets wrote in Tuscan Italian as well. Their writings were widely read and admired throughout the country and helped establish the Tuscan dialect as the standard written language of Italy. Tuscan Italian did not become the standard conversational language, however, until the middle of the twentieth century.

Today, though standard Italian is used in schools and in government, many people are beginning again to speak their local dialect at home or to mix it with the official language. For example, in standard Italian, the word "white" is *bianco*. But for people in Genoa, the word is *giancu*, while the people of Naples say *iango*, and those in the toe of Italy's boot use *asipro*.

In addition to all the dialects, small numbers of people in some border areas speak non-Italian languages. These include German, French, Albanian, and Serbo-Croatian. The mixing of languages and dialects has made it hard to create a sense of national unity.

Hand gestures, facial expressions, and body language are all vital parts of Italian speech. Conversations are lively mini-dramas of movement. In the city of Naples, for example, there are thirteen ways of saying no through gestures and expressions.

SAY IT IN ITALIAN

Here are some common words and phrases in standard Italian:

Good morning, good afternoon, or a general hello	*Buon giorno* (bwohn-JOOR-noh)
Hi, or so long	*Ciao* (chow)
Good evening	*Buona sera* (BWOHN-ah SAY-rah)
Good night	*Buona notte* (BWOHN-ah NOHT-tay)
How are you?	*Come sta?* (KOH-may STAH?)
Fine, very well	*Molto bene* (MOHL-toh BAY-nay)
Thank you	*Grazie* (GRAH-tsyay)
Yes	*Si* (SEE)
No	*No* (NOH)
Excuse me	*Scusi* (SKOO-zee)
Good-bye	*Arrivederci* (ah-ree-vay-DEHR-chee)

Numbers:
1. *uno* (OO-noh); 2. *due* (DOO-ay); 3. *tre* (TRAY); 4. *quattro* (KWHAT-tro); 5. *cinque* (CHEEN-kway); 6. *sei* (SAY); 7. *sette* (SET-day); 8. *otto* (OHT-toh); 9. *nove* (NOH-vay); 10. *dieci* (DYAY-chee)

The Italian alphabet is a little different from our English alphabet. There are no letters *J, K, W, X,* and *Y*. *J* has become popular with the use of the word "jeans," but in Italy, it is sometimes pronounced "yeans."

One reason for this animated speech is said to be the Italian love of drama. People try to bring out the feeling or emotion of every statement. Gestures are so important that there are even dictionaries of the many Italian movements and expressions!

Country Life

Only about one quarter of the Italian people live in rural areas. Most of these live in farm villages and market towns in southern Italy and on the islands of Sicily and Sardinia.

Poor soil, uneven rainfall, and hills and mountains combine to make life hard for most southern farm families. Over the past century, the hardships have led millions to emigrate, or move, to other parts of Europe or the Americas. And since 1950, more than 5 million people have moved to the industrial cities of northern Italy.

Farm families grow wheat and vegetables and raise a few goats, pigs, and chickens to meet their own needs. Groves of sturdy olive trees provide them with a cash crop—products to sell in the markets. In fact, Italy is one of the largest producers of olive oil in the world.

At this street market in the northern city of Bologna, shoppers can buy produce grown in the rich farmland of the Po River Valley.

In the past, southern farm families lived in tiny cottages or hillside caves. Often, they had to share these cramped quarters with their farm animals. But, in the past forty years, the Italian government has worked to improve conditions in the south. Roads have been paved, schools built, and electric power developed. New, low-cost housing has made living conditions much more comfortable. Most families now have radios and television, and many own automobiles.

Country life in the north presents a far different picture. The fertile soil of the Po River Valley, and a few smaller river valleys, produces lush fields of wheat and corn. There are also huge rice paddies. Vineyards provide grapes for Italy's famous wines, and the mountain valleys are grazing land for cattle, sheep, and goats. While farmers in the hilly south often must rely on donkeys, those in the north can use modern farm machinery.

Life in the Cities

Since 1950, Italy's economic boom has transformed the country from a poor agricultural land into a prosperous industrial nation. Nearly three quarters of the people now live in cities or large towns. Most of these are in the northern and central regions.

The cities were once isolated by the mountains. Now they are connected by modern express highways called *autostrade* (out-oh-STRAH-day). Within each city, however, traffic slows to a crawl. Cars, trucks, and buses must maneuver through narrow, twisting streets that are many centuries old. Each city has a ring of modern suburbs. The center of each city, though, is a wonderful blend of the very ancient, the merely old, and the modern. Gleaming office buildings of steel and

In Italy, many city apartments have balconies like the ones photographed on this street in Milan.

glass share space with magnificent cathedrals, churches, and palaces built hundreds of years ago.

Most city dwellers live in apartments. The apartments tend to be small but are neatly furnished. Almost every apartment has a balcony, which people use for growing plants, socializing, and sometimes for hanging laundry. Other city residents have private homes on the outskirts of town.

The northern cities have modern factories that produce steel, clothing, electronic goods, and automobiles. Many of Italy's industries, like the Fiat automobile works, are world-famous for their sleek, ultra-modern styling. In addition to factories, city workers are employed in department stores, shops, and restaurants. Others work in offices, banks, and government agencies.

Every village and town in Italy has a central square, or piazza. The cities have several. A favorite pastime for Italian families is a stroll, which is called the *passegiata* (pah-say-JAH-ta), to and around the piazza. There, young people meet friends, families exchange news, and neighbors chat. Because

Residents and tourists relax on the famous Spanish Steps of the Piazza di Spagna in Rome.

it often is in front of a church, the piazza is also the center of activity on festival days.

Every city has other places for meeting, shopping, and eating. In Milan, for example, people gather at the Galleria Vittoria. This is an ornate, glass-ceilinged shopping arcade built in the 1870s. In Rome, the many beautiful fountains are favorite meeting places, along with the Spanish Steps.

The Importance of the Catholic Church

More than 95 percent of all Italians are Roman Catholics. Most take their connection to the Catholic Church very seriously, although only about one in three attends church regularly.

Italians think of their country as the home of the Roman Catholic Church. And, indeed, Vatican City, in the center of Rome, has been the capital of the Church for nearly 2,000 years. (Today, though, it is an independent state.)

The Church helps people throughout the country. For example, it runs some of the best schools. It also operates many hospitals and homes for the elderly and infirm. The parish priest is very important in the daily lives of many people in the south and on the islands.

Both people and pigeons flock in large numbers to the piazza in front of St. Mark's Cathedral in Venice.

There are a few Protestant churches in Italy, especially in the north. The Jewish people have a long history in Italy. Today, there are a number of synagogues where they worship. Some are hundreds of years old.

Families spend a lot of time together in Italy, where a weekend outing often includes treats at a café.

3

FAMILY LIFE, FESTIVALS, AND FOOD

The Italian Way of Life

On a warm, sun-filled afternoon, an Italian family plans a holiday meal. The whole family is coming—aunts and uncles, grandparents, cousins, nieces and nephews. Because the apartment is small, the family plans to celebrate at a neighborhood restaurant. With lots of food, talking, and laughing, the meal will last the entire afternoon. Afterward, everyone will take a leisurely stroll. For Italian families, this is a perfect way to spend a day.

Family Traditions and Change

Italians have strong family ties. A family in which grandparents, cousins, aunts, and uncles are closely involved with one another is called an extended family. In the past, all over Italy, members of an extended family lived near one another, often under the same roof. They could count on one another for help and support. This tradition continues in many of the farm villages of the south, Sicily, and Sardinia.

Modern city life, however, is changing family traditions. Today, most households consist of only the nuclear family—the husband, wife, and children.

But, even though relatives no longer live together, Italian families manage to maintain strong ties. Sons and daughters who have moved away come back whenever they can for family gatherings. There is also great respect for older family members. Italians will do all they can to care for their elderly parents and grandparents.

The roles of family members are changing dramatically. In the past, Italian families were patriarchal—that is, the father was the unquestioned head of the household and his word was law. Boy children were future family heads. Girls were taught to remain in the background and to provide the strength that held the family together. Women, however, exercised a quiet power behind the scenes. They had an influence on every important family decision.

The two sexes are on a more equal footing in today's Italy. Girls now receive the same education as boys, and they are much more willing to speak up. More and more, women are working outside the home, many of them in professions such as education, communications, and health care. Today, for example, nearly one third of Italy's doctors are women.

Holidays, Holy Days, and Festivals

In Italy, there are many occasions for community celebrations and for family gatherings. Italians observe several national holidays. One is Liberation Day (April 25), commemorating the end of World War II, when the Germans were defeated.

Most of the holy days that are celebrated in Italy follow the calendar of the Roman Catholic Church. Since most

Italians are Catholic, they celebrate Christmas, Easter, Ascension Day, and many other Christian holidays. There are also regional variations, since every city and town marks the feast day of its patron saint.

One of the most important events in the life of most Italian boys and girls is receiving their first Holy Communion. This special religious event, called a "sacrament," usually occurs when the boy or girl is eight years old. It is a time for a joyous family celebration.

The season around Christmas, the day Jesus Christ was born, is a time of great joy in Italy. Many families attend church on the

In a small town in central Italy, the feast day of San Gerardo is celebrated with band music played in a brightly lit gazebo.

nine evenings before Christmas. Churches and homes are decorated with *presepios*, or Nativity scenes. A family's *presepio* often contains beautiful, hand-carved figures of the Holy Family—the baby Jesus, Mary, and Joseph.

Some families exchange gifts on Christmas morning. But the traditional gift day is January 6, Epiphany. On this occasion, Catholics celebrate the day the Three Wise Men presented gifts to the infant Jesus.

LA BEFANA, THE GIFT GIVER

In Italy, the traditional giver of Christmas gifts is not Santa Claus, but *La Befana*, the good witch. The name comes from *L'Epifania*, the Epiphany.

According to legend, the Three Wise Men invited Befana to visit the infant Jesus with them. But she got there late because she had to finish her housework! Each year on January 6, she returns on her broom with gifts for the children.

In the villages, a man may dress up as an old woman to play the part of Befana. In the cities, the main piazza is the setting for a colorful toy fair. Children can enter little houses for a chat with Befana, the Three Wise Men, or even Santa Claus. Santa is becoming more popular in Italy. Many children write their letters of hope for presents both to him and to Befana.

A few weeks after Epiphany, the start of Lent is celebrated with *Carnevale*, which means "farewell to meat." For three days, there are parades, puppet shows, plays, and bands. These events usually take place in the piazza.

Carnevale is followed by the forty solemn days of Lent. This is when Christians remember the crucifixion of Christ. Lent ends with Easter, when Christ's resurrection, or return to life, is celebrated.

A number of festivals include fireworks. On the day before Easter in Florence, for instance, people enjoy the *Scoppio del Carro*—the "Blowing up of the Car." The day marks the resurrection of Christ. A car loaded with fireworks is pulled in front of the cathedral. As the Mass (a Catholic service) ends, a rocket in the shape of a dove swoops down from the cathedral along a wire that stretches all the way to the car. Boom!—a huge fireworks explosion announces that "Christ has risen!"

Every city and town also has its own unique religious festivals. One of the most famous is the *Palio*. It is held in the city of Siena twice every year on July 2 and August 16. Ten of the city's seventeen districts are chosen to enter a horse and rider in a wild race held to honor the Madonna, the mother of Jesus. The day begins with the riders leading their horses into the church for a blessing at the altar. This is followed by a parade in which people wear costumes of the Middle Ages. There are bands and knights in glittering armor. The horse race is three times around the main piazza (about 2 miles, or 3.2 kilometers). Mattresses are laid down to protect riders on dangerous turns. The winner receives the *Palio*, a large banner bearing a picture of the Madonna.

Many festivals, especially in Sicily, are known for their puppet shows. It was an Italian, Carlo Collodi, who created one of the most famous puppets when he wrote the story of Pinocchio.

Whatever the occasion, every festival includes food, music, and dancing. The celebration lasts far into the night.

The townspeople of Ravello watch a parade in honor of the Pentecost, which is celebrated on the seventh Sunday after Easter.

Food, Delicious Food

In Italy, a good meal is an important part of the enjoyment of life. Italians like to use simple and fresh ingredients. There are few supermarkets in Italy, because people prefer to shop at local markets, where the food is fresh.

Bologna is known for its sausages, such as those hanging from the ceiling of this local salumeria, *or delicatessen.*

A café in Venice offers a selection of tempting pastries.

Breakfast is a simple meal—usually just a roll and coffee or warm milk. The main meal is served around 1:00 P.M., although today, many working families have to wait until evening. On weekends and holidays, this afternoon dinner will last from two to four hours. The evening meal is usually a light snack.

The first course of a family dinner is usually an antipasto—a platter of cold cuts, olives, and cheese. This is generally followed by a pasta dish (although rice or a dish made from cornmeal are common substitutes in the north). Pasta is simply a dough made of eggs and wheat flour. Spaghetti is one form of pasta; there are at least 200 other forms. Some of the pasta shapes have colorful names, like *cannelloni* ("big pipes") or *cappelletti* ("little hats"). Those who like spaghetti with meatballs may be surprised to learn that the dish is rarely served in Italy, except around Naples!

After pasta, the next course is meat or fish, along with vegetables. This is followed by a green salad and then dessert. The most common dessert is fresh fruit, often served

FETTUCINE ALFREDO

Of all the Italian pasta dishes, fettuccine with butter and cream is one of the most famous, and also one of the easiest to make. Fettuccine are flat noodles. You can buy fresh fettuccine in the refrigerated section of most supermarkets, or you can use a package of the dry noodles. Pasta, Italian style, should be cooked *al dente*, which means tender but firm "to the bite."

Ingredients:

1/4 cup butter
1 cup heavy cream
salt and pepper

1 pound fettuccine noodles
1/4 cup grated Parmesan cheese

1. In a large frying pan, melt the butter. When the butter foams, add the heavy cream. Add a dash of salt and pepper. Let this simmer for about 2 minutes to thicken a little.

2. In a large saucepan, cook the fettuccine in boiling, lightly salted water, according to the package directions.

3. Drain the fettuccine and place them in the skillet with the butter and cream. Sprinkle the grated Parmesan cheese on top. Stir the noodles and sauce thoroughly over low heat for about 30 seconds, so that all the noodles are coated with the sauce.

Serve at once, along with extra Parmesan cheese for those who wish it. This makes about 4 servings. With bread and a salad, you have a quick and easy Italian meal.

with two or three kinds of cheese. On special occasions, the family may have a cake or pastries from a local bakery. And some people think that Italian ice cream, or gelato, is the tastiest in the world.

Clothing Styles, Old and New

The people of Italy love to dress well. In fact, Italy is one of the world's leading producers of clothing, shoes, and leather goods. Designers in Milan, Florence, and Rome create fashions that are widely followed throughout the world.

These musicians on the island of Sardinia, wearing richly decorated costumes, are having fun at a festival.

While designer shops in Italy's cities cater to the very wealthy, dressing well doesn't have to mean wearing lots of expensive clothes. Most Italians wear clothes that are stylish but inexpensive. Young people favor jeans, T-shirts, turtle-necks, and sweaters.

Throughout the year, Italy's many holy days and festivals give people the chance to dress up in the colorful styles of the past. The most popular traditional clothing seems to be that of the Middle Ages and the Renaissance—brightly colored cloaks and plumed hats for men, and flowing gowns for women. Other traditional costumes include peasant garments, with puffy white sleeves, vests, and bright sashes or shawls.

Students learn about Italy's rich heritage as they explore the city of Bologna on a class outing.

4

SCHOOL AND RECREATION

Learning and Leisure

All Italian children are required to attend school from ages six to fourteen. However, children usually attend kindergarten when they are three or four years old and stay in school past age fourteen.

Most children go to public schools. About 10 percent attend private schools; these are usually run by the Catholic Church. Elementary school lasts five years. Students then go on to three years of middle school.

Young people who want to continue their education beyond middle school have a number of choices. Students who hope for a career in music or art can go to an arts high school. There are other kinds of high schools as well. There are schools for business careers, for training in science and technology, and for college preparation. In addition, some teenagers decide to become apprentices. An apprentice learns from a master craftsperson the difficult skills needed to become, for example, a glass blower, leather crafter, or potter.

Students from any five-year high school can go on to college, but first they must pass a tough examination. There are more than thirty colleges and universities in Italy. Many are run by the government and have low tuition. One of the oldest universities in Europe is located in Italy: the University of Bologna. These days, more and more young people plan to go to college in the hope of qualifying for the best jobs.

A School Day

If you were attending an elementary school in Italy, you would probably walk or ride your bike to school, although school buses are becoming more common. The children gather in front of the school door a little after 8:00 A.M., boys on one side, girls on the other. In most schools, the students wear uniforms, such as a blue smock and white collar, with a thick red bow for girls and a loose tie for boys. Everyone is chattering about the difficult homework or about the great TV special the night before about Mount Etna, Sicily's smoldering volcano.

A teacher arrives to unlock the door, and everyone rushes noisily to one classroom or another. Teachers and students have given each room a cheerful appearance by covering the walls with maps, murals, and the students' own artwork.

Italy spends a large portion of the government budget on education. Nearly all of it goes for teachers' salaries rather than for new school buildings or the purchase of new books. Because Italy has so many well-trained teachers, each classroom has fewer than twenty students.

When the teacher enters the room, all talking stops and the children stand as a sign of respect. The lessons begin promptly at 8:30 A.M. The first lesson of the day may be geography. The teacher may show slides of the coast of the Ligurian Sea. This coast includes the city of Genoa, birthplace of the explorer Christopher Columbus.

After geography comes history, followed by the day's writing lesson. On one day, the teacher may ask students to write stories about Guglielmo Marconi. He was an Italian scientist whose inventions made radio broadcasting possible in the early 1900s.

After the history and writing classes comes math, with its tough homework questions. Then a priest may enter the classroom to talk about a coming holy day. The last lesson may be Italian grammar, and again there is a lot of homework.

At 12:30 P.M., the bell rings, ending elementary school for the day. While some elementary schools have a longer school day, most hold classes for half a day, including Saturday.

Few schools have a cafeteria or a gym. Children come to school for the serious business of learning. After classes, most have the whole afternoon to look forward to—along with the homework.

Time for Fun

After school and the big afternoon meal at home, Italian children still have a few hours of daylight for outdoor fun. They may join friends for a long bicycle ride or take part in bike races around a park.

Any kind of ball will do for kicking. A circle of boys and girls will stand on a street corner for hours, trying to keep a small rubber ball in the air, using only their feet, knees, and heads. These informal games help build the skills needed for *calcio* (CAL-choh), or soccer, Italy's most popular sport.

A group of boys kicks around a soccer ball after school. Calcio, *or soccer, is Italy's favorite sport.*

BOCCE: BOWLING, ITALIAN STYLE

On Sundays, Italians are fond of the slow drama of the game of *bocce* (BOCH-ay). The game, a form of lawn bowling that dates back to ancient Rome, used to be played mostly by elderly men. Now Italians of all ages enjoy it.

Bocce is played on a narrow court of finely crushed cinders or closely clipped grass. One player rolls a small ball, called the *pallino*, to the far end of the court—about 60 feet. The two teams each roll four larger wooden balls, trying to get as close to the *pallino* as possible. The course is lined with wooden planks, and expert players are skilled at bank shots off the boards. A brilliant bank shot will knock an opponent's ball out of the way and leave the thrower's ball closest to the *pallino* to score a point.

On cold or rainy days, children enjoy indoor board games like *Reversi*. *Reversi* is like tic-tac-toe, except that there are thirty-two Xs and Os, played on a board with thirty-six squares. Hand or finger games are also popular, the favorite being *morra*. In *morra*, each of the two players makes a fist, then, at a signal, shows any number of fingers and calls out a number. The number called is a guess of how many fingers the other player is going to show. If your guess is right, you win a point. *Morra* goes faster and faster as the excitement builds. Soon, both players are shouting the numbers.

In the evening, children usually join their parents for a relaxing walk around the piazza or along a shopping street. Part of the fun is buying a snack from one of the pushcarts. You can choose small, thin pizzas, chestnuts, sausage, even snails or octopus. Or you might prefer to have a delicious gelato (ice cream).

Most Italian families go away for vacation, and the favorite places to go are Italy's famous beaches. Many of the beaches have boardwalks with restaurants, food stands, and a variety of shops.

The Pleasure of Sports

Calcio, soccer, is the country's number-one sports passion, both for playing and watching. There are more than 6,000 soccer clubs scattered throughout Italy, and pick-up games are played in every park. On Sunday afternoons from September to June, thousands of people jam Rome's Olympic Stadium and other arenas. Matches to qualify for the World Cup, with more than 130 countries involved, create the greatest excitement. Feelings run high at these matches. A player or team can be booed out of town for poor play, but the star players are treated as heroes.

Bicycle racing and automobile racing also create great excitement. The Tour of Italy bicycle race starts in Milan and winds through much of the country. A favorite automobile race is the *Mille Miglia*, or "Thousand Miles." Like the Tour of Italy, this race covers a long distance over Italy's twisting mountain roads. The Italian Grand Prix is also popular. This annual race involves specially built "formula" cars, with their sleek lines and open cockpits.

Basketball and baseball draw more people every year. In both sports, the professional Italian teams are allowed to sign a limited number of American players.

Winter sports also enjoy great popularity. Many people like hockey, ice skating, and bobsledding, but the favorite is skiing. In the Italian Alps, people can ski all year, and even Sicily, in the south, has good winter skiing. Ever since the

The Tour of Italy bicycle race has been an annual event since the early 1900s.

Winter Olympic Games were held at Cortina in 1956, more and more Italians have taken up skiing. It has become a popular winter vacation sport for families. Italy's most beloved sports hero, Alberto Tomba, known as *La Bomba* ("The Bomb"), has electrified crowds throughout the world with his reckless charge to victory in ski races.

47

Italy's churches are filled with works of art, such as this centuries-old mosaic in St. Peter's Basilica in the Vatican.

5
THE ARTS

Blending Past
and Present

In 1966, the Arno River overflowed its banks, flooding the city of Florence. Even while the floodwaters were rising, hundreds of people struggled through the frigid, waist-deep water on a rescue mission. Their goal was to save as many of the city's famous paintings as possible. Masterpieces from the Renaissance as well as modern works by lesser-known painters were at risk. After the floods, even artworks that were badly damaged were slowly and carefully restored to their original magnificence.

The incident reflects the Italian people's deep love and respect for artistic beauty. This fondness for art extends to sculpture, architecture, and fine crafts as well as painting.

Painting, Sculpture, and Architecture

Italy has some of the world's best-known art museums and galleries. But Italians also enjoy seeing painting and sculpture in more natural surroundings. The famous mural *The Last Supper*, by Leonardo da Vinci, for example, remains on the wall of the convent in Milan where he painted it.

Some of the greatest sculptors in history, such as Michelangelo (1475–1564) and Gianlorenzo Bernini (1598–1680), made magnificent statues, not for galleries, but to grace the fountains and piazzas of Italy's cities. Bernini also applied his genius to designing churches, altars, courtyards, and even bridges that help to make Rome one of the world's most beautiful cities.

Two thousand years ago, the artists of the Roman Empire created beautiful paintings on the walls of houses, temples, and other buildings. In a similar way, Christian artists of the Middle Ages adorned the walls of churches and cathedrals. In the late Middle Ages, Giotto di Bondone (1267–1337) revolutionized artistic styles by giving his paintings a feeling of depth, or perspective. The painters of the Renaissance—such as da Vinci, Michelangelo, and Raphael—followed Giotto's lead to create the realistic-looking paintings of that period. One of the most amazing examples is Michelangelo's painting of the ceiling of the Sistine Chapel in the Vatican.

Throughout Italy, restaurants, shops, and public buildings are decorated with paintings. Some are by well-known

The scenes from the Bible that Michelangelo painted on the ceiling of the Sistine Chapel in the Vatican are among the greatest works of the Renaissance.

The dome of Florence's beautiful cathedral was designed by the Renaissance architect Filippo Brunelleschi.

artists. Most, however, are by unknown men and women who keep alive the tradition of surrounding people with beautiful images.

Italy is also famous for its architecture, especially in its churches and cathedrals. The cathedral in Milan, for example, called the *Duomo*, is one of the world's largest and most beautiful churches. Built in the style of the Middle Ages known as Gothic, its outside walls are decorated with more than 2,000 life-size statues. St. Peter's Basilica in the Vatican is even larger. This church structure has parts designed by both Raphael and Michelangelo. Building the Basilica took more than a century.

Crafts: A Continuing Tradition

The sight of laundry hanging from rooftop lines is not unusual in Italy. But in the northern town of Cremona, you are more likely to see rows of violins hung to dry. Cremona is the center of one of Italy's many remarkable handicraft industries. For more than 400 years, Cremona's craftspeople have followed in the footsteps of great violin makers like Antonio Stradivari (1644–1737). Each violin is carefully crafted out of seventy two pieces of wood—some of it aged for ten years—then finished with thirty coats of varnish. These violins, along with cellos and violas, are considered the finest in the world.

The glassblowers on the island of Murano are famous for the beautiful chandeliers and glassware that they produce in their studios.

Other Italian crafts are also built on time-honored techniques. On the island of Murano, near Venice, glassblowers use highly secret methods developed 600 years ago to produce exquisite vases, goblets, and chandeliers. They also make intricate glass beads embedded with colorful chips. In villages throughout Italy, leatherworkers create beautiful purses, belts, shoes, and gloves. In larger cities, such as Florence, handmade leather goods are recognized for their elegant styling.

Every city and town in Italy has open-air markets. There, family-owned stalls offer a dazzling array of handcrafted items. At some stalls, you will see hand-painted pottery in an endless variety of lively colors and patterns. Some of the best ceramic items, including tiles and mosaics, are made by potters in mountain villages.

At other stalls, there are displays of handmade lace, including beautiful tablecloths, shawls, and bridal veils. A little farther on in the market, there will be baskets, handbags, and hats made of straw or raffia (a fiber from a palm tree). Both in market stalls and in small shops, you will find lovely examples of gold and silver jewelry. Some of the bracelets, rings, and necklaces are copies of ancient designs. Others are very modern.

Literature and Film

The writers of Italy have been creating outstanding literature for more than 2,000 years. Ancient Rome produced such poets as Virgil, Horace, and Ovid. Julius Caesar was known for his writings about his military exploits. Other Romans, like Cicero, were famous for their public speeches.

During the centuries that followed the fall of the Roman Empire, religious writers continued to write only in Latin.

ITALY IN ARTS AND LETTERS

Here are six of Italy's many famous artists, writers, and scientists. Their achievements had a great influence on later generations.

Dante Alighieri (1265–1321), poet. Dante's long narrative poem, *The Divine Comedy*, is considered one of the finest literary works of all time. It describes the poet's journey from Hell to Purgatory and then to Heaven.

Marco Polo (1254–1324), traveler and explorer. His only book, *The Travels of Marco Polo*, told wondrous tales about Cathay (China) and the empire of Kublai Khan. It was the first account by a European of China's amazing civilization. It helped to launch Europe on an age of exploration by influencing such adventurers as Christopher Columbus.

Leonardo da Vinci (1452–1519), Renaissance painter, sculptor, architect, engineer, and inventor. His two most famous paintings are *The Last Supper* and the *Mona Lisa*. His immense curiosity led him to draw designs for things far ahead of his time, including a flying machine and a submarine.

Michelangelo (1475–1564), Renaissance sculptor, painter, architect, and poet. He is best known for his sculpture called the *Pietà*, for towering statues of the biblical figures David and Moses, and for his painting of the ceiling of the Sistine Chapel in the Vatican. He is considered one of the greatest artists of all time.

Galileo Galilei (1564–1642), scientist, astronomer, and mathematician. Galileo constructed the first lens, or refracting, telescope for examining the heavens, and he proved that the earth revolves around the sun. He was condemned by the Catholic Church for denying that the earth was the center of the solar system. (He was, of course, proven right by later scientists.) He was also the first scientist to test theories through experimentation.

Giuseppi Verdi (1813–1901), composer of opera. He produced such works as *Aida*, *Rigoletto*, and *Otello*. Verdi developed what became known as "Grand Opera," with its lavish stage sets and elegant costumes.

Later, in the fourteenth century, Dante's *The Divine Comedy* was the first masterpiece written in Italian.

Modern Italian writers have continued the traditions of the past. In the twentieth century, five Italians have won the Nobel Prize for Literature—considered the highest tribute an author can receive. Two of the Nobel Prize winners were from Sicily. A third, Grazia Deledda, based her work on the folktales of her native Sardinia.

Many people outside of Italy are more familiar with the country's movies than with its literature. When World War II ended in 1945, much of Italy lay in ruins. There was little money for movie making. Despite these problems, the postwar period became the golden age of Italian cinema. *Rome: Open City* (1945) and *The Bicycle Thief* (1948) are still regarded as classics for their stark images of people struggling to overcome the ravages of war.

Music

At a festival in southern Italy, villagers dance an ancient, fast-paced folkdance called the tarantella. In northern Carrara, stonecutters measuring a block of marble hum an aria, or song, from an opera. And in Venice, a young boatman, called a gondolier, gives his version of a popular romantic song as he steers his gondola along the Grand Canal. Music is everywhere in Italy, from the religious music of the Middle Ages known as Gregorian chants to rock songs.

Of all musical forms, Italy is best known for opera. Opera is a dramatic story told through music. This complex musical form was first developed in Florence in about 1600. During summer opera festivals, huge crowds gather at outdoor sites. The rest of the year, they flock to opera houses, such as the famous La Scala in Milan, where they can hear their favorite operas. Such well-known works as Gioacchino Rossini's *The Barber of Seville*, Giuseppe Verdi's *Aida*, and Giacomo Puccini's *Madame Butterfly* have thrilled opera lovers the world over for more than one hundred years.

Italians approach opera with intense emotion. Many opera-goers know every note played by the orchestra or sung by the soloists and chorus. They cheer mightily for a great performance. But even the most famous stars, including the legendary Enrico Caruso, have been booed and hissed for badly sung passages.

Performances at Italy's grand opera houses, such as Milan's famous La Scala, pictured here, are filled with enthusiastic audiences.

Folk dancers step to a lively beat on one of Italy's many piazzas.

Italians are fond of other kinds of music as well. Every region has produced its own folk music, for example. Many of the traditional songs have now been collected on tapes and CDs. In the cities, modern music is more popular than folk songs. Jazz musicians, such as Mike Melillo, often cut records with American jazz artists. Pop music ranges from upbeat tempos, such as the songs of Alice Eliser, to romantic tunes, rock music, and rap. Italians also listen to American pop songs and to the old-style songs of such famous Italian Americans as Frank Sinatra and Liza Minelli.

Italians' taste in art and music is like the people themselves: varied and vibrant. But whether in the city or the countryside, the north or the south, they never fail to fascinate!

Country Facts

Official Name: *Repubblica Italiana* (Republic of Italy)

Capital: Rome

Location: a peninsula jutting into the Mediterranean Sea from southern Europe. In addition to the Mediterranean, the peninsula is formed by branches of that sea: the Adriatic Sea, in the east; the Ionian Sea, in the south; the Tyrrhenian Sea, in the west between Sicily and Sardinia; and the Ligurian Sea, north of Sardinia. France forms Italy's northwestern border. Switzerland and Austria lie to the north and Slovenia to the east.

Area: 116,304 square miles (301,225 square kilometers). *Greatest distances:* east–west, 130 miles (209 kilometers); north–south, 708 miles (1,139 kilometers). *Coastline:* 2,685 miles (4,321 kilometers)

Elevation: *Highest:* Monte Rosa in the Alps, 15,203 feet (4,634 meters). *Lowest:* sea level

Climate: great temperature variations, depending on altitude. The north generally has hot summers and cold, moist winters. In the south, the climate is warm to hot, but with cold winters in the mountains; it is dry much of the year.

Population: 58,100,000. *Distribution:* 74 percent urban; 26 percent rural

Form of Government: democratic republic

Important Products: *Natural resources:* asbestos, bauxite, marble, sulfur, zinc, mercury, and some oil and coal. *Agriculture:* cheese, grapes (wine), lemons, oranges, peaches, wheat, corn, barley, olives, figs, almonds, and chestnuts. *Industries:* automobiles and trucks, clothing, electronic equipment, office machines, glasswork, ceramics, jewelry, oil refining, and chemicals

Basic Unit of Money: lira; 1 lira = 100 centesimi

Language: Italian is the official national language, with many regional dialects. Small minorities speak French, German, Albanian, and Serbo-Croatian.

Religion: at least 95 percent Roman Catholic, with small numbers of Protestants and Jews.

Flag: a rectangle with three vertical sections: red on the outer side, white in the center, and green closest to the pole. Often called the *Tricolore* ("Tricolor").

National Anthem: *L'inno di Mameli* ("Hymn of Mameli"), by Goffredo Mameli, an Italian patriot

Major Holidays: New Year's Day (January 1), Epiphany (January 6), Easter, (varies from year to year), Feast of St. Joseph (March 19), Liberation Day (April 25), Labor Day (May 1), National Day (June 1), Assumption (August 15), All Saints' Day (November 1), Armistice Day (November 11), Immaculate Conception (December 8), and Christmas (December 25).

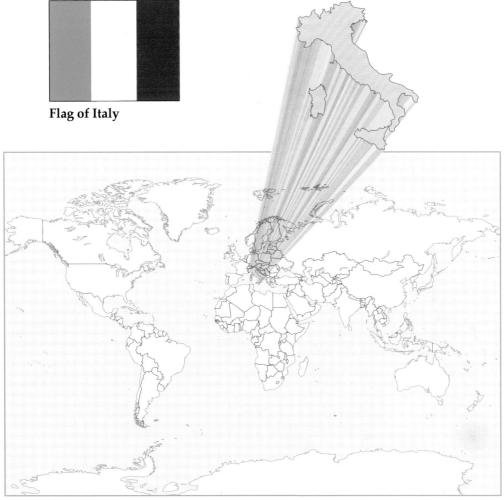

Flag of Italy

Italy in the World

Glossary

apprentice: a person who works with a master craftsperson to learn the skills of a craft, such as weaving or glassblowing

aqueducts: pipes or elevated structures used to carry water over long distances

autostrade (out-oh-STRAH-day): highways

city-state: an independent state made up of a city and surrounding countryside

Dark Ages: the period from the fall of the Roman Empire, A.D. 476, to the start of the Middle Ages, about A.D. 900, when the knowledge of ancient Greece and Rome was nearly lost

dialect: a form of language that is spoken in a particular area

gladiators: trained fighters who fought against each other or against wild animals in the Colosseum of ancient Rome

guerrilla warfare: the strategy of fighting a war or revolution with hit-and-run tactics and avoiding a pitched battle

legions: the main fighting units of the ancient Roman army, made up of between 3,000 and 6,000 soldiers

Middle Ages: the period from about A.D. 900 to the 1300s, a time when many great European cathedrals and churches were built.

Palio: a festival held in the city of Siena twice each summer, featuring a horse race around the main piazza

passegiata (pah-say-JAH-ta): a walk

patriarchal family: a family in which the word of the father is supposed to be unquestioned

peninsula: an area of land surrounded by water on three sides

piazza: a city, town, or village square, often in front of a church

presepio: the word means "crib" but refers to the traditional Nativity scene of the Holy Family at Christmas

Renaissance (REH-nuh-sahns): the great flowering of art and culture from the 1300s to about 1600. The Renaissance began in Italy and later spread throughout Europe. Artists and thinkers were inspired by the ideas of the ancient Greeks and Romans.

Risorgimento (ree-SOR-jee-men-toh): a word meaning "rising again" and referring to the nineteenth-century movement to make Italy a unified and independent nation

Vatican City: a small area within the city of Rome that is the center of the Roman Catholic Church. Although it lies within Italy, the Vatican is an independent state.

For Further Reading

Bisel, Sara. *Secrets of Vesuvius: Exploring the Mysteries of an Ancient Buried City*. New York: Scholastic, 1993.

Butler, Daphne. *Italy*. Madison, New Jersey: Raintree Steck-Vaughn, 1992.

Clark, Colin. *Journey Through Italy*. Mahwah, New Jersey: Troll, 1994.

DiFranco, Anthony. *Italy: Balanced on the Edge of Time*. Minneapolis, Minnesota: Dillon Books, 1983.

Hubley, John and Penny Hubley. *A Family in Italy*. Minneapolis, Minnesota: Lerner, 1987.

James, Ian. *Inside Italy*. New York: Franklin Watts, 1988.

McClean, Virginia. *Pastatively Italy*. Memphis, Tennessee: Redbird, 1994.

Winter, Jane Kohen. *Italy*. New York: Marshall Cavendish, 1993.

Index

Page numbers for illustrations are in boldface

About the Author

"One of the great things about books is that they can carry us to every corner of the world. We can also travel back in time, visiting people and places from recent years or the distant past. I hope you enjoy this book's journey across both space and time," says David C. King.

Mr. King is a historian and an author, who has written more than thirty books for young readers. In addition to books about foreign countries, he has written stories and biographies in American history. He and his wife, Sharon Flitterman-King, live in the village of Hillsdale, New York. They welcome visitors.